Written by Chemise Taylor

A book on calming strategies and emotional regulation

Copyright © 2026 by My Skills Books

Published by My Skills Books

All rights reserved. No part of this publication may be reproduced, distributed, or transmitted in any form or by any means, including photocopying, recording, or other electronic or mechanical methods, without the prior written permission of the publisher, except in the case of brief quotations embodied in critical reviews and certain other noncommercial uses permitted by copyright law.

First Printing, 2019.

ISBN: 978-1-951573-66-9

www.myskillsbooks.com

I can be calm

I can
be cool

When I get upset, I know what to do

I can take 5 deep breaths

1 2 3 4 5

I can count to 10

6 7 8 9 10

I can talk to a parent

I can talk to a friend

I can think positive thoughts

I can ask
for a break

I can count backwards from 10

10   9   8   7   6
5   4   3   2   1

I can write dots or scribble on paper

I can hum a song

I can write how I feel in a journal

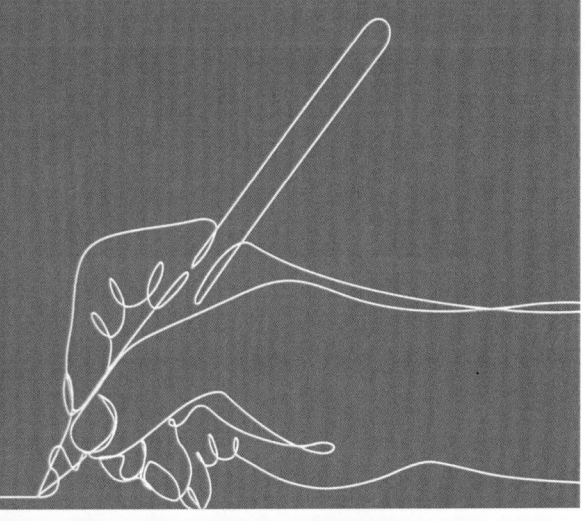

I can ask to go for a walk

I can do it!

It's no big deal.

I can say a calming phrase

I'm okay.

I am smart.

I can remember I am in control and can think things through

I can listen to music

I can color or draw a picture

I can do one of my favorite hobbies

QUIET ZONE

I can go to a quiet place to calm down

I can play with water, sand or a sensory toy

I can say how I feel in a calm, nice manner

I can squeeze a stress ball.

I can think of things that make me happy or laugh

I can exercise

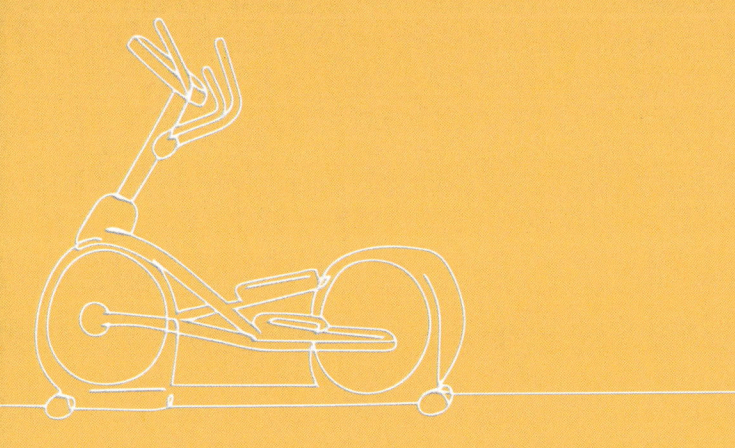

I can do a silly dance

I know things won't always go my way and it doesn't seem fair

But getting upset doesn't get me anywhere

When I get upset I know what to do

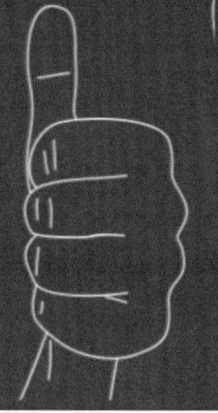

I can try to stay calm and keep my cool

Book Details

Story Word Count: 254

Key Words: Calm, Cool, I, Can

Comprehension Check

- What are 5 ways to stay calm?
- What calming strategy do you like the most?
- What calming strategy do you like the least?

Reading Award

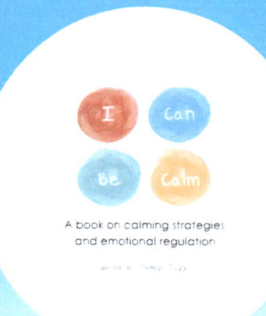

This certificate goes to:

_____

for reading "I Can Be Calm"

Good Job!

More books, apps and resources at myskillsbooks.com

www.ingramcontent.com/pod-product-compliance
Lightning Source LLC
Chambersburg PA
CBRC090450090526
44586CB00033BA/93